v v v

The Fall of Autumn

v v v

S. Libellule

v v v

Introduction

Of all the seasons, autumn is by far my favorite. Having grown up in New England, I was blessed with seeing the full glory of fall with all its foliage. The vivid reds, yellows, and burnt oranges set the woods ablaze in color. I always associate the coming of autumn with a return to school, a re-commitment to learning and wisdom. This then makes it a season of the mind. It is also a transition from the warmth of summer to the snowy cold of winter. For me, this an annual reminder of the passage of time and the how death is another year closer. It is always a season of internal reflection about my life and what I hope to do with whatever time I have left.

Dedication

This book of poetry is dedicated to one of my favorite poets, Robert Frost. I encountered his poems as a student in high school. He spun such poetic wisdom in his verse and was a consummate professional. His homespun Yankee wisdom was always so clear and moving to me. I keep a collection of his poetry on my desk in a place of honor.

Contents

The Fall of Autumn

Funny how a single leaf
can so foretell grief
as it is blown drab
scratches my concrete slab

Once more colorful leaves
now tattered sleeves
strip bare the autumnal day
while winter makes his way

Chills my frosted breath
this cold harbinger of death

[Autumn Dons Her Best]

Autumn dons her best

while cool winds come from the west

to join the gala

Autumnize

It is the perfect way to accessorize
add a little splash of color
some pretty seasonal panache
trying to blend in
while you seek to stand out
golden golds
scarlet reds
burnt oranges
all set the world ablaze
as you once again autumnize

[Autumn Leaves Its Hint]

Autumn leaves its hint

in the faint glint of each tint

kissed by cool breezes

Fallen

Autumn falls like a curtain
again making me certain
that winter whispers are now
every closer
for even the breeze
rustling the trees
warns of stronger winds
of colder days
while I now feel the chill
of a defiant will
stirring my ink

turning the page

Waning

These cool autumn days
have lost their blaze
as the sun shows his age
shedding pale light
surrenders more to each night
while these dappled trees
hear rumors on the breeze
of longing winter nights
too cold for even the moon
who veils herself too soon

mourning for the fall of autumn

Autumn Apples

I sit in my sunroom
with autumn in full bloom
colorful leaves outdoing
the blossoms of spring
taking the time
to compose a little rhyme
next to the bright white bowl
full of nice sliced apples
red delicious
living up to their name
then... eating them fast
for I know they won't last
knowing they will brown

just like all of these leaves

Autumn Crush

Those autumn days
were set ablaze
with such lovely flames
orange, yellow and red
contrasted
against the tranquil blue
chilled in the fall air
we never seemed aware
of how it would all burn out

September is...

This month after August
wedged in so tight
in between the sunlight
of summer and fall

Makes me recall
this time of year
all I do fear
all I do still cherish

Heading back to school
as the weather did cool
pulling out the sweaters
finding the thick wool socks

Listening to the clocks
a little closer
as they do chime
implore more rhyme

Measure the waning days
in more careful ways
knowing deep inside

winter will no longer hide

[Each tree now shivers]

Each tree now shivers
as autumn begins its fall
the leaf breaks its bond

[Falling Autumnal]

Falling autumnal

painted leaves so like sleeves

float again downward

Deciduous

The jigsaw puzzle leaves
prove each tree believes
in this joyful game of life
the mystery of all things

An Impressionistic scene
of a watercolor so serene
the day is now painted
in its vibrant perfection

Still a mere blur to the eye
beneath a sapphire sky
these living days may pass
without a thought

Relentless hours tick down
without making a sound
while calendars turn the page
the cycle reaches its repetition

Until each arboreal crown
begins again to fall down
drape the ground below
so that each of us may know

Autumnal

Sol once again
shifts
his royal arc
softening his gaze

While I sit
transcribe
decipher
the lengthening shadows

Paying notice
to no real timekeeping
just another tick mark
in balmy September sand

Then wondering again
as I often do
about his true position
on my sundial...

Heralding mid-morning
highest noon
or

his final most casting

Leafed

The hillside is dappled
with the hallmark
of chilled colors
so many hues to choose

In so many ways
the ever-shortening days
entice
still mystify

As I stroll along
in search of a song
or maybe some verse
to play with these words

Capture each leaf
in a line that is brief
as crisp as autumn
with its cool air

In this life of compare
of contrast
searching for all that list
beyond the pretty foliage

To Build a Fire

Inspired by "To Build a Fire" by Jack London

Such a deep primal desire
to build a fire
gather up black lichens
strike the flat flint

Smell that first smoke
feel the first choke
of wet warmth
on cold dry lungs

Stepping back in time
long before rhyme
had the power to warm
the gift of healing

When woman listened to her heart
knew she was a part
of the great Arctic circle
the web of all living things

As that first moose call
trumpeted the arrival of fall
echoed in the turning trees
the poetry of the autumn breeze

Foliage

Each brown leaf
now knows autumn is just a thief
wearing her bright disguise

[Autumn Has Fallen]

Autumn has fallen

along with the first red leaf

preparing for grief

Waning Sun

The warm liquid gold
is getting colder
turning ever pale
while sun starts to sink
starts to dip
just like the sharp tip
of my pen

ready to commence again

[Such Painted Sleeves]

Such painted sleeves

under these most dappled of leaves

fall is in fashion

Autumn Pyre

These scattered words

remain

like so many blown
leaves
trapped within the eaves
in the old rustic barn
orange and red flaming hues
among these autumn blues
as I face a windy west
pulling up my stiff collar

enduring

another tumbling sundown

Windblown

This grey autumn day
looms while it again brooms
these freshly fallen leaves
upon this uncaring breeze

Reminding all the pretty trees
how beauty will not last
everything fades into the past
no matter plumage or pedigree

While seeds of Death are sown
upon a wintery wind now blown

Autumnticity

It happens every year
whenever winter is near
Autumn paints all her leaves
to camouflage how she grieves

Sharing secrets on the breeze
she confides only in the trees
reveals all the lies she has told
before the coming of the cold

Unveiling the depth of her pain
while the daylight begins to wane
while her season come to an end
as each swirling leaf does blend

For there is a sweetness in despair
seeing my breath upon the air
knowing my words will linger
I trace this frost with my lost finger

Brook

It is the time
between times
between seasons
having no need of reasons

As the brook swells
with each secret it tells
so silvery and slow
as it meanders soft

Carrying my dreams aloft
down the hillside
leaving behind all pride
on its way to the sea

Once again reminding me
in a simple way minding me
quenching so much more
than a parched imagination

As I hear the faint trickle
my ear feels the tickle
of a subtle whisper
disguised in autumn rhyme

Debris

The neighbor's yard is covered
with brown leafy debris
as far as I can see
husks of defeated autumn
strewn all about
leaving no doubt
that November has arrived
with all of its barrenness
making me again confess
my dread of the dead of winter

Autumn Daydreams

What do leaves dream about
when they finally do flout
all of the rules
changing their verdant shades

Show off all their fall luster
along with such bluster
on a breezing autumn day
that now seems out of season

Looking more like oil paint
than any true feint
to fool everyone
except this poetic mind

Even as the waning sun
has finally begun
to make his wintered plans
heading south for warmer inspiration

While I start out on my way
on this crisp October day
not knowing what I will find
only all that I shall leave behind

Sagittate

The lone leaf is crisp
the dead leaf has fallen
on the ground
without a sound

Autumn always remains
relentless
with its chilling breeze
defeating all the trees

One leaf at a time
coloring it bold
coloring it bright
before the dead of night

Despite all its points
its razor-sharp edges
the perennial battle is won
before it has begun

Leaving this omen
this solitary reminder
how the arrival of fall

awaits us all

Septembre

French for "September"

This month likes to rule
while the weather turns cool
the leaves again begin
to don their fall plumage

While the sun starts to fade
soft light filles the glade
sends a message
shows a sign

Making me resign
to this perennial truth
known since my youth
that winter is inevitable

This season of the soul
will always exact its toll
seek its due
in exchange for wisdom

For in order to learn
we must be willing to burn
all the dead fallen trees
to then listen to the breeze

A Saturday in September

The wall calendar says fall
so too the bald meteorologist
now that the latest equinox
has passed into the past

Still I sit here again
befuddled...
my mind so muddled
by the warm humid day

While the sky is all
cemented
so gray in its hue
not a trace of any blue

As I feel so out of mind
outside of time
in need of some rhyme
to help me again recall

Of the Her artistic flair
wild vividness everywhere
laced with a lingering chill

as rainbowing leaves tumble

Novemberist

What can I say
I was born this way
born in a melee of fall

as if I were meant to falter
tripping upon each altar
getting caught up in it all

embracing every single sect
with its own brand of genuflect
as I heed each plucked Siren call

never ever thinking twice
before any mortal self-sacrifice
before I don the black pall

so I celebrate another November
in the hopeless hope to remember
self-portraits fading upon the wall

Autumn Afternoon

Now is that time
between times
within autumnal rhymes
that I do so love

The lazy warm hollow
of the afternoon
when the paled sun
has begun its arced dive

While I curl up snug
on my leather couch
feeling the touch
of my down comforter

While the apple crisp
bakes ever slow
filling the room
with a cinnamon bliss

Outside vagabond leaves
ride the cool breeze
sporting patchy colors

trying to catch the wind

Scathe

Scars are the very roadmap
to my dark past
the only thing to last
all of these wicked miles

Each still beguiles
in its own curvy way
says what it has to say
in my own personal braille

For pain and travail
are the guardrails of my life
a double-edged knife
to cut and be cut

Yet here I still strut
fretting upon this page
in this neo-post-modern age
left empty of any blue ink

Standing upon the brink
of an unavoidable fall
hearing the Sirens' call
autumn with its perennial trap

[Autumn Again Blooms]

Autumn again blooms
while winter always still looms
whispers in the breeze

Autumn

The cool breeze is faint
while Nature starts to paint
Her annual masterpiece
one leaf at a time

More beautiful than rhyme
set high up in the tree
meant to mesmerize me
enchant the whole forest

Red, orange and gold
each with a story now told
in an arboreal way
only poets can understand

A poetic sleight of hand
right before my eyes
eliciting my sighs
warming my tender heart

Wondering where to start
to begin the first line
in search of the divine
offer up this most humble poem

[Autum wears her best]

Autumn wears her best
keeps her leaves close to her chest
hiding their true hues

Burnt Orange

It is the color of these leaves
the true shade of the glade
when autumn comes to call
with its deep secrets to share
passed on down by the trees

Whispered poetry on the breeze
filling an early autumn air
with a dire omen for us all
about his scythe with its blade
sharpened by the one who grieves

Palette

This happens every fall
Right before us all
She has to use all these hues
In the hope it won't be seen

How She has run out of green

[Such Autumnal Bliss]

Such autumnal bliss
when the September winds kiss
all the blushing trees

Scattered Leaves

These dead scattered leaves
are like red tattered sleeves
in the fabric of my day
tossed about in all my doubt
painted by light shadow
dappled in bright sunlight
just so I may write all I see
on an autumn afternoon free
of all usual pretense
my present becomes your past tense

October Skies

October skies are the place
for cool goodbyes
letting leaves just fall
like so many unrequited

tears

Autumn Chill

The brisk stroll aches
thus laden so true
revealing my breath
like the frozen dew

Gone are the fickle
warm summer days
luring me to bliss
with glistening rays

Shaded ever safe
beneath my willow
your deft quill scratching
soft lap my pillow

Each cerulean sky
I then did ignore
preferring instead
angelic allure

Till emulous fall
stole away love
by unfurling doubt
with skies ashen above

Deciduous

Do some leaves then decide
to dress up in bright colors
then just

drop

floating to the ground
with barely a sound

surrendering

to cool autumn winds
leaving all the trees
ride the October breeze
having lived out the year

only to now fall like a tear

Falling

I see how She grieves
for the fallen autumn leaves
wishing She had not

painted them all ablaze

Hills of Gold

The time is just past
highest noon
on a waning day
this early September

While I try to remember
innocence
never ending childhood
frolicking in the wood

Chasing lofty dreams
beside mossy slippery streams
beneath a golden canopy
created just for me

Moments do come and go
they speak as they show
laced with lessons to learn

while memory does burn

Blustery

Despite these long sleeves
I join the blown brown leaves
in their autumn chill

Falling

Brittle autumn leaves
left the victim of thieves
stealing all of the color
from my once warm cheeks

Autumn Falls

It truly does fall in so many ways
how this shortening of days
is felt in the chilled breeze
then by all these painted trees

Who drop their gilded leaves
before every one then grieves
another loss to coming winter
how weak branches will splinter

While each leaf floats to the ground
thus defeated without making a sound

Falling

Funny how in this time of year
I always feel her coming near
in the chilling breeze
how she seduces with such ease

While the leaves wear their plume
allowing poetry to have the room
within each stanza and line
in accordance with her design

For Autumn always loves to show
all she still prizes within the flow
of a cool September day
when steals my breath away

As memories from so long ago
whisper now in the winds that blow
recall Gypsy days when I would roam
living my life as if written in poem

Cinnamon

Chilly November memories
fog my breath
fog my mind
as I now succumb

Golden maple leaves
long sweatered sleeves
running through the plaza
your warm hand in mine

Stopping at the cafe
the only ones outside
cupping our mugs
in both hands

The smell of cinnamon
filling the air
our love without a care
with each creamy sip

A taste on the lip
for another sweet kiss
such autumnal bliss
high on this spice of life

Inked

I live in this world of ink
left always on the brink
of another timed line
another rhymed write

Often late into the night
beginning once again
with just parched paper and pen
awaiting some omen or sign

A subtle hint at Her design
all She has to say
in Her most cryptic way
about the meaning of things

Like counting arboreal rings
to be sure of the current age
interpreting whispers sage
carried gently on autumnal winds

While all promise rescinds
to hid deep within the tide
all of these mysteries now linked
with this wet poetry now inked

Novembered

I was born in November
on a rainy day I cannot remember
too warm for snow
finding me too dry to cry
all these dead brown leaves
still left for one who grieves
not for what was lost
but for what was won
missing out on the summer sun
each and every year
shielded beneath the shade
of a Damoclesian blade

Winnowing Wind

"Thy hair soft-lifted by the winnowing wind" ~ Keats

This autumn breeze is just a tease
a sampling of what is to come
blowing about my hair
in this day of devil-may-care
mischief does love its company
with so much to divulge
so much to keep secret
leaving me here left speechless
only an unrung bell
still awaiting the knell
each gust a telltale splinter

the cold calling card of winter

Evergreens

They are the arboreal poets
of these silent trees
chronicling with ease
the passage of time
within the metric of rhyme

Witnessing each fall
recounting it all
beginning each new spring
with a new iambic ring
yet recite these wintery regrets

Shower of Leaves

I watch them fall
before autumn even arrives
while summer still thrives
at least for a few more weeks

Perhaps it is because
this particular year
Death is now here
holding my reluctant hand

I carry her with me now
joining in this journey
from cradle to gurney
how it must then end in dust

Still I see their beauty
lightly painted hues
all the color this imbues
as they fall... far too soon

Pile of Leaves

Some are strong oak
others sweet maple
mixed together here
by undiscerning winds

Each fell all alone
floating to the ground
now a great big mound
but brown and brittle

As time continues to whittle
away at these remaining roots

Autumn Rain

It is warm for early November
as if I am meant to remember
this particular place
this temperate time
jot it down in disposal rhyme
as clouds of light grey
shroud the midday
I listen to the rain try to explain
autumn with its noble fall
what it now portends for us all

Debris

The pasture is strewn
with brown leaves blown
huddled in groups
beneath the baring trees

Each unwilling to render
any form of surrender
give up
to the march of seasons

With so many reasons
to remain
to abstain
from any such debate

While we all wait
for that first single flake
to finally make
its fluttering appearance

Nature to give her clearance
for the arrival of winter
as my thoughts do splinter
cracks in a foreboding ice

Brown Leaves

How each one always grieves
for the loss of verdant green
a boldest theft by these thieves
who now come and go unseen

Autumn Leaves

They are more than a sign
or proof of the divine
in their splendid garb
their resplendent colors

Painted on the broad trees
dried by a fall breeze
that carries along
a seasonal truth

About the passage of time
the truncation of rhyme
occurring right now
not the why but the how

While I again take stock
fixated on the clock
on the calendar
on the year

Wonder if it is near
knowing it is closer
while the sand shifts
as my life once again sifts

Frost

I saw it today
how it sugar coated
the normally dewy grass
gleaming in the lamplight

Giving the world a hint
a sign
of what is to come
with winter and its cold

All that we behold
as the year dies
surrenders again
to a new shiny calendar

As I search for something sage
to relearn
to again discern
from the tiny ice crystals

That swiftly pass by
avoiding any when or why
as I speed headlong
towards a frosted reckoning

October

This evil month truly
vexes me
hexes me
with its own curse

For better or worse
the dropping of leaves
is like the shredding of sleeves
the tattering of the trees

While even in the breeze
there is a whisper
a faint hint
of the fading glint of sun

Fooling almost everyone
that winter is not coming
so keep the guitar strumming
keep the party going

Even though a wind is blowing
each brittle brown leaf
like some silent thief

stealing away our innocence

Palette

I often do wonder
does She ever lick
Her long slender brushes
before she paints
Her resplendent autumn

This sweeping mural
that replaces verdant days
in such colorful ways
always making me
smile

With this artistry
fully surrounding me
always deeply inspiring me
to take another long
breath

Cherishing the day
in a most poetic way
stubby pencil in hand
crisp page beneath
awaiting my muse

Finally able to choose
the first spilt line

inspired by the divine
in all of its beauty

all its glorious verity

Autumnal

Tragic how birch tree leaves
those verdant sleeves
begin yellowing, showing their age
as chilly evenings now engage

As Sol does wane
they struggle in vane
to resist the clarion call
of an existential fall

Falling for Autumn

She returns alone each year
always making it clear
how she will not stay
after she has had her play

Painting all of these leaves
to wear them for her sleeves
she begins her slow undress
leaving me here left to confess

While I await her last first kiss
surrender to her cool bliss
as she reaches down below
everywhere I dare not go

Letting herself then linger
caressing with every finger
this longing chilled skin
its slow surrendering to sin

Disarming as only she can
every single woman and man
who hears her Siren call

finally seducing them all

September

A coolness whispers in the air
taking me back to there
when autumn was a time to return
another chance to again learn
the lessons of the day
the paths along my way
as I now long for a look
within another cracked book

Autumn

She always fills my dreams
with her poetic schemes
Autumn paints all of her leaves
with a beautiful camouflage

While blowing me a kiss
making sure she will miss
her allure is so pure
her temptation so complete

As if dancing upon a chilling air
she lives a life devil-may-care
never worrying about winter
never longing for spring

With her scent upon the breeze
always so willing to tease
out my confession of true love
my professing a deep desire

Until it is again time for her to go
right before the first flakes of snow
can land softly upon her face
covering up any remaining trace

Autumning

It is what I seem to do
when my summer is through
as I feel the cooling fresh air
warn me to again beware

While these leaves change hues
spread now their seasonal news
about looming days ahead
about this upcoming dread

About another year gone by
without any real answer why
these days lose their luster
despite any reason I muster

How the weather truly knows
far more than it dare shows
about these secrets left to find
within an ever-troubled mind

Autumnal

The seasons come then go
as if meant to show
the extant urgency
of the now

How my passage of days
in the usual ways
is somehow different
somehow more poignant

Even the cool breeze
rustling the trees
whispers this message
issues this warning

So clear in this morning
with the cool dew
remembering what is true
about being so alive

As I again try to thrive
breathe deep the breath
stave off any fear of death
as the first leaf now turns

First Leaf

Funny how this colorful first leaf
reveals this perennial thief
along with his calling card
this cool breeze across my yard

For autumn comes each year
makes it perfectly clear
how summer is over
along with its bee bumbled clover

While the season becomes unhinged
I watch the leaves turning tinged
in their red, orange and gold
as their falling future is now told

Since another year has passed
the rays of September will not last
as the sun begins to wane
making the forecast truly plain

But in the end I do know
how even I will one day go
no more laps around the track

as I will no longer be coming back

In Late September

This time out of time
no longer summer
is not quite fall
kept in seasonal limbo
with leaves not knowing
what to do
while even a sky of blue
is more than a little sad
so it is always here
that I gin up a tear
glance both ways
forward then back
for the things I still lack
that I always remember
in late September

Unforgotten

All the things I recall
are still faded leaves of fall
painted in watercolor
left out in the rain

As if seen through a tear
with some facets still clear
as a precious gem
these keepsakes I reclaim

What then to cherish
which memories to let perish
on the dulling pyre
of ever-fading embers

So many days I did live
still somehow able to give
each of them a name
each a most treasured place

But now the days dwindle
by the Fates with their spindle
not a single thing now regrettable

with this one life... unforgotten

The Fall of Autumn

This is the time of year
when smile weds tear
here where the present melts
into the buttery yellow foliage

Leaving only what is left behind
as both heart and mind
seek to reassure my soul
that this trail was traveled well

While the sunlight grows faints
as the season does paint
a most vibrant landscape
before these aging eyes

With the days now cut short
without any real retort
I accept that winter
is not content to stay away

In the end I chose this path
unafraid of its aftermath
as blowing leaves sprawl
within this autumn with its fall

Leaf

Autumn always reminds me
that Death is a thief
as I tally every leaf
when it is finally blown free

Slowly floating to the ground
see-sawing back and forth
it rides cold winds from the north
landing without making a sound

As this foliage lets go of its dreams
plummets helpless so it seems

Each painted with the colors of fall
they now pirouette before us all

A foreshadowing of our own end
while these defeated colors now blend

[I listen to trees]

I listen to trees
while they confide in the breeze
autumn's betrayal

Swollen Sky

I again sit here wondering why
beneath this swollen sky
why the clouds refuse to rain
the heavens will still not cry
despite the greyness of this day
the words no one dare say
aloud or in verse
be neither blessing nor curse
until the fall of these leaves

allows for each who now grieves

Falling Backwards

It seems I do it every year
when I remember November is here
set all the clocks back
relive that haunted hour
from one to two
only to find nothing new
about the world
about myself
for that is the thing about time

always defying reason and rhyme

Dangle

It hangs up so high
having so very far
to fall…
to succumb to autumn

Relentless is this wind
the raw breeze
up in the trees
laced with a winter chill

This epic battle of will
of one against
the raging season
the uneven odds

Occurring every year
reflecting every fear
felt
or yet to be felt

The direction we head
each of us
in our own special way

each and every day

Aftermath

These scattered leaves
strewn like tattered sleeves
tell it all...
tell the aftermath of fall

How once colorful hues
become yesterday's news
casualties of brutalizing time
with its chronology of crime

Returning every year
as if just to make it clear
Death will not relent
no matter the solaces we invent

For finally in the end
winter never seems to bend
never repent
with its wicked weather sent

Meanwhile a haunting breeze
whistles through these bare trees
given me its fair warning
in this season of my mourning

Harvest Moon

She performs for just three nights
models all of her gravitating delights
before these cool September skies
mends all of these broken lies
only to make them finally true

Knowing nothing less will do
while the leaves continue to turn
as the chaff continues to burn
with winter coming far too soon
for this fleeting harvest moon

Leaf

Autumn always reminds me
that Death is a thief
as I tally every leaf
when it is finally blown free

Slowly floating to the ground
see-sawing back and forth
it rides cold winds from the north
landing without making a sound

As this foliage lets go of its dreams
plummets helpless so it seems

Each painted with the colors of fall
they now pirouette before us all

A foreshadowing of our end
while these defeated colors now blend

Autumn's Fall

I await the turning of the leaves
the shedding of these colorful sleeves
that foretells this time of change
this moment meant to now rearrange

Reflecting on all these past deeds
while I anticipate future needs
remember how the current year
is but a calendar awaiting its tear

For I once again now find
myself in the season of mind
where reason and doubt
can finally have it out

The Fall of Autumn

Each season has its reasons
For coming to an end
For coming to a close
After sharing all its knows
With any receptive mind

So each new fall I still find
As the darkness then grows
The autumnal breeze blows
Whispers a message to send
Warning all the other seasons

Bluster

Fall has some nerve
its own homegrown
arrogance...

using its tragic magic
turning these noble leaves
from green to orange to brown

before they all fall down
in a splendid parabolic defeat

it vanquishes summer
every single year
relishes every conquered tear

yet Autumn always forgets
that like the leaf its reign is brief

forgetting winter is right behind

[Autumn Hates to Lose]

Autumn hates to lose

all those many splendid hues

withering palette

Autumn and Its Fall

The bastion of this season
is always well beyond reason
in how it seems to linger
how it again points its finger

To the passage of the years
the concatenation of my fears
I only seem to truly feel
when the ending year seems real

Knowing I am a little further on
ticking off another chilly dawn
on my way to my own conclusion
desperate in my search for any allusion

While I do long for some surprise
in the form of useful alibis
something to finally make sense
of a life with a dwindling future tense

Yet I settle again into this write
authenticate these feeling contrite
prepare to finally face it all
the end of Autumn and its fall

Falling into Autumn

I always seem to fall into autumn
as if I am unaware
of the chill in the air
of all that will then come

Another chance to plumb
as deeply as I dare
caring as much as I care
re-feel feelings now numb

As I realize the end of the year
is just a matter of time

Just as every unshed tear
awaits the perfect rhyme

While we all still do fear
every tolling bell with its chime

Whisk

Sometimes it seems this way
on any given day
this tumble
this jumble

My thoughts race
my doubts face
in all directions
for all to see

The meltdowning me
here on display
alone yet wanting to play
the part of normalcy

Feeling so strong
with a need to belong
in the fold
walk so centered

Not live splintered
my mind sintered
by these autumnal extremes
longing for more poetic dreams

[One lone leaf denies]

One lone leaf denies
all that wicked winter tries
only to then fall

[Autumnal Skies]

Autumnal skies
are again filled with the chill
of all it denies

[Falling into Fall]

Falling into fall
I hear the clarion call
of December's end

[Autum with Its Fall]

Autumn with its fall
Once more reminding us all
Of winter's revenge

[The Fall of Autumn]

The fall of autumn
is the last thing I recall
before winter wins

Autumn Rains

Autumn rains do weep
themselves to sleep
to dream of winter snows

[Loose as a Fall Leaf]

Loose as a fall leaf

awaiting an autumn thief

stealing more each year

Chilled Wisdom

There is a calming in the air
that makes me again aware
of the turning of seasons
of the culmination of my reasons

Lessons under the summer sun
have finally just begun
to now sink in
allow me once more to begin

For the passage of the years
exacted its toll of tears
these battles won and lost
make me still carry all their cost

Yet there is a peace found here
making everything so clear
as I unfold this Gypsy way
listen closely to what it may say

Written within this cool breeze
I decipher the mysteries of the trees
hear all that they now profess
within all this autumn coolness

[Am I now alone]

Am I now alone
the only one who still grieves
for this pile of leaves

Septembering

I now face another September
kept alone as if to remember
the warmth of that embrace
the smooth contours of your face

Memory is funny that way
beckoning the lonely mind to play
games it cannot win
how an end dare not rebegin

Yet I find myself lost again
holding only my pen
in this wake of black ink
feeling feelings that make me sink

Drowning once more
in a love I thought was pure
one that was meant to last
until our future became our past

But I guess that is how it goes
when autumn now blows
scatters all the leaves
of those wearing hearts on their sleeves

Auric

The day is dipped in gold
quite the sight to behold
by these old weary eyes
with all their fading alibis

For Autumn has taken the fall
sacrificing herself for us all
one bright leaf at a time
just to spice up some rhyme

So, how then to begin to pen
not write the same things again
set this cool moment apart
capture this affair of the heart

Somehow delve down deep
be able to shelve dreamless sleep
wade now into the warm stream
of some lasting poetic dream

Where poems write themselves
fill up endless eternal shelves
as I wrap myself up in the metaphoric
live a life in a world forever auric

[A Fresh Pile of Leaves]

A fresh pile of leaves
makes me roll up my sleeves
dive into Autumn

Sheen

The freshly cut grass is a show
vibrant and verdant all aglow
glistening with silver dew
listening once more anew

While summer slowly retreats
another season now completes
its three month perennial run
with the waning September sun

For it is always at this time of year
that I feel deep truths coming near
a promise of true revelation
in the form of poetic consecration

As if all I am meant to know
will somehow finally show
itself to me
so that again I might then see

A wisdom beyond the ages
enough to fill these tattered pages
convince the world sight unseen
with this erudite iridescent sheen

Autumnal Breeze

I do love to feel the breeze
whispering through the trees
sharing their autumnal rhymes
from more vernal times

When all the leaves were green
and all that could be seen
was the promise of spring
hope and wonder in everything

Before summer with all his pride
with a wintered morality kept denied
insistent on strutting upon the stage
never cherishing this present age

But as for little old me
I would still rather be
listening to each fallen leaf
commiserate with its lonely grief

For I know every poem will end
never making it around the bend
never reaching forever...
even if I am so damned clever

Autumn's Fall

Like all things that do relent
she is also meant to break
meant to feel the fall
from the height of beauty
to the depths of this despair

Autumn has sadly seen it all
from the betrayal of the leaves
their turning, falling one by one
never returning back home
except within lines of poem

First to Fall

It is perennially the first to fall
that single leaf seems to tell it all
spiraling towards the ground
making hardly any sound

Yet it happens every year
while it gins up another tear
about the shortening of days
the looming ending of our ways

For whether it be leaf or man
this was always Winter's plan

Autumnal Duel

It is always I against me
Who I am versus the one you see
Meeting again here every year
In this season most sincere

Joining all of these fallen leaves
Along with anyone who still grieves

Season of the Mind

I have come to find
Autumn to be the season of mind
As the days become ever short

Leaving me left to resort
To some deep pontification
In the hope of true illumination

While I reflect upon the years
Cataloguing all my tears
Just to add them to my ink

Sitting quietly as I again think
About the meaning of such things
About what lessons this fall brings

Harvesting

This autumn is a harvest time
while words drop like leaves
to be so gathered up in rhyme
only to be discarded as sheeves

The Fall of Autumn...

I await the turning of the leaves
the shedding of these colorful sleeves
which foretells this time of change
this moment to then rearrange

Reflecting on all of these past deeds
while I anticipate future needs
remembering how the current year
is but a calendar awaiting its tear

For I once again now find
myself in the season of the mind
where certainty and doubt
can finally have it out

Autumn Bliss

Autumn is a joyous celebration
a magical inkantation
inspired poems from all around
fills the fall air with all their sound

The kiss of this cool breeze
reciting poetry from these trees
once again finds me lost
among these leaves left tossed

With each new stirring feeling
I again am still revealing
all of the things I do adore
loving them now ever more

While She paints all of Her hues
with a delicacy to then choose
the colors of this season
unveiling every true reason

Such contentment beyond compare
as I breath in the chilly air
feeling the soothing kiss
of this crisp autumn bliss

Autumnic

It is a certain state of mind
always leaving me to find
what it leaves in the foliage
what clues fall to the ground

How such messages convey
all that they have to say
within their bright colors
within their brief example

Reminding me once again
of the urgency of the pen
to capture the moment
while all these feelings foment

Foliage

Her such perfect camouflage
prevents any real triage
about how badly the maples bleed
or how much the yellow birches cede

A better understanding
from this world cold and demanding
yet even I still now fall
end up joining the rest of them all

Fooled by Autumn with her skills
feeling the first blown September chills

Early Autumn

Autumn comes early way up here
chilling even the most heartfelt tear
for Alaska keeps her deep secrets
right next to all her cherished regrets

Feeling that the first felt chill
warm up the sentimental quill
I pen lines of love
recite them from high above

While at this higher latitude
I adopt a most different attitude
letting go of foolish things
quit pursuing these brass rings

As I breathe in the fresh air
recite a silent prayer
to be carried on the breeze
then translated by the trees

Then I mourn the summer sun
how the cold weather has begun
leaving a light snow dusting
leaving me a little more trusting

Autumn Breeze

I do love to feel the breeze
whispering through the trees
sharing their autumnal rhymes
from more vernal times

When all the leaves were green
and all that could be seen
was the promise of spring
hope and wonder in everything

Before summer with all his pride
with a wintered mortally denied
insisted on strutting upon the stage
never cherishing the present age

But as for little old me
I would still rather be
listening to each fallen leaf
commiserate with its grief

For I know every poem will end
never making it around the bend
never reaching forever...
even if I am so damned clever

An Autumn Fall

Even with the first falling leaf
I feel this perennial grief
for life needs to always remind
all that we will leave behind

How this very here and now
will one day meet the plow
become buried underground
muffling every sobbing sound

Despite these vivid hues
I know that they will lose
to the heavy hand of time
living on only in some rhyme

Yet what does this now teach
in a lesson still within reach
some wisdom to then behold
while my life continues to unfold

[An Autumn Poet]

An autumn poet
loves to write all of her lines
beneath pining pines

The Poetry of Leaves

I weep for everyone who grieves
within the poetry of leaves
how all these vibrant hues
seems to hide all of their blues

When a raw chill fills the air
laced with a hint of despair
reminding one and all
about the sad omens we recall

For beauty can truly hurt
when our eyes cannot avert
from the wonder we cannot forestall
the lonely dignity of fall

While each of us still prays
in our many varied ways
trying hard to understand
leaves blowing like desert sand

[The Lone Harvest Moon]

The lone harvest moon
always seems to come too soon
for those in the chaff

A Fall Farewell

Fall is a perennial farewell
a reoccurring fare thee well
with a bow from the trees
a cool courtesy from the breeze

Leaving me here left again
with fresh ink to fill my pen
a brand-new ache in my heart
to help my poetry again restart

For I once more feel this pain
as my sunlight begins to wane
stretching all of our shadows
beyond what each of us knows

Since we are running out of time
in a poem chock full of rhyme
aware how these stanzas will end
how similes and metaphors will blend

Departing a life lived long and hard
Autumn now leaves her calling card
while I commence now to quinter
fallow the field for a dark winter

Autumn Wise

It happens every single year
every laugh and each tear
must then be tallied up
in a half-empty, half-full cup

As I wonder why the Harvest Moon
always seems to come around too soon
while the days pass ever faster
despite all that is left to master

For the turning of the leaves
share more than each perceives
a sage moment to be unfurled
revealing much about the world

As Fall becomes the season
the one of mind with all its reason
always such the surprise
making only the poet autumn wise

After the Fall

Autumn leaves all fall
as if meant to warn us all
about the end of days
the termination of our ways

How the long cold winter
makes weak limbs splinter
under the burdening wet snow
just to make sure we each know

No matter what we do
every lie finally becomes true

[Autumn will now fall]

Autum will now fall
a performance for us all
as leaves pirouette

Autumn Blush

I savor the cool rush
while the leaves blush
their perennial shade of red
sharing a poetry left unsaid

For even these trees
now recite with such ease
the flowing chilled lines
of Her autumnal designs

As giddy springtime dreams
join sparkling summer streams
in my memory's collage
build up this fall decoupage

While I travel merry on my way
into a refreshing September day
since I know deep in my heart
how all my sorrows will now part

A Dusting

This white crown of snow
again lets me know
the relentlessness of winter
as autumn begins its splinter

For way up here
wintery weather is always near
with a deep chill in the air
painting trees with a colorful flair

As I feel the silent fall of it all
creatures large and small
hear the poetry in the breeze
the inevitable coming of the freeze

So, I embrace this sacred time
consecrated in thoughtful rhyme
meant to firmly take hold

before the arrival of a true cold

Coniferous

Their forest green is clearly seen
up here all year round
no matter the looming sound
of wicked winter winds

While each cracked branch reminds
me of these true lessons learned
from each wildfire burned
how life up here is always hard

Allows me to now discard
all of these many doubts
my own uncertain whiteouts
that still try to stand in my way

For no matter what they say
there remains a rustic truth
so many would deem uncouth
which echoes in these trees

Whispering raw poetry in the breeze
from those learned days behind
recited again so I may now find
a clarity is all that is pristine

Autumnally

It always seems Autumn falls
in her own time
makes her own rhyme
branch upon branch, line upon line

According to her deft design
she paints all of her cool leaves
adorns each tree with its sleeves
in such vibrant autumnal hues

Allowing her to spread the news
celebrate each and every year
while knowing its end is near
that Winter is ever looming

But also of springtime blooming
the return of budding life
this perennial cycle so rife
with all of its beckoning calls

Setting Sun

I love how the setting sun
has once again begun
to remind me
of all I left behind me

Another summer day gone
one more once upon
a time...
desperately in search of rhyme

All these waning sun rays
recall lost glory days
when I was young and strong
always so willing to sing along

These places I have been
tattoos and scars on my skin
that I often do retrace
trying to recapture some grace

Since I know the days ahead
have their share of hope and dread
but I have yet to ever regret
a single sunset

A Mindful Season

Autumn is always the time
for the most introspective rhyme
a time to contemplate
how the hour grows ever late

With every page I now turn
I watch the candle further burn
making a puddle of wax
while these metaphors do tax

For every taper is brief
since death is a clever thief
distracting us with colorful leaves
so we then forget all who grieves

While each cool fall breeze
will both warn and tease
about the urgency of now
of both the sickle and plow

So, I once again reflect
about how this is so circumspect
with me never knowing when
I will run out of ink for this pen

Made in United States
Orlando, FL
27 September 2023